MOSCOW
AND
LENINGRAD

MOSCOW
AND
LENINGRAD

MARTIN HÜRLIMANN

78 PICTURES IN PHOTOGRAVURE
9 COLOUR PLATES
AND 9 LINE DRAWINGS

LONDON
THAMES AND HUDSON

FIRST PUBLISHED 1958

TRANSLATED FROM THE GERMAN BY DAPHNE WOODWARD

CONTENTS

PLATES

MOSCOW AND LENINGRAD

THE SETTING

From time immemorial the word 'Moscow' has symbolized for the West not only the capital of Russia, but a whole strange realm, an alien world of gruesome tyranny, glittering-gold cupolas and peals of Easter bells—the cradle of Ivan the Terrible's Muscovy; the scene of Boris Godunov's tragic end; the spot where the splendour of imperial coro- nations alternated with days of horror in which not only the Tsar but the flower of the aristocracy might be slaughtered together with countless burghers and peasants; the birthplace of the youngest empire of the Old World; the city whose conflagration plunged the mightiest conqueror of modern times into bewilderment and defeat and before which Hitler's tremendous war machine, too, came to a halt. The romantic image of this Moscow, built up from history books, novels and operas, has a place in the background of the Western consciousness. But before it there towers nowadays the highly topical picture of the stronghold of Soviet Com- munism. 'Moscow' has become a fateful word in government circles throughout the world, a challenge to the most ancient national traditions. It denotes one of the alternative types of life between which it is the destiny and duty of every human being to decide.

A book such as this cannot go deeply into the theme of Moscow as an aspect of world politics; but it cannot entirely ignore that theme. In studying the monuments that give character to this city and to its sister- city on the Neva, Russia's second capital, we follow the course of history and try to discover certain constant features which recur even today and may play their part in helping us to understand the full significance of the term 'Moscow'.

The journey to Russia is an adventure for a Westerner even nowadays, so the present writer and five of his fellow-countrymen, all interested

The Red Square in the seventeenth century: the Patriarch passes through in procession.
Left, the Cathedral of St Basil; in the background, the Kremlin.

Chr Rothgießer Husum fecit

From *Beschreibung der moskowitischen und persischen Reise*, by Adam Olearius, 1647.

chiefly in the arts, had no hesitation in seizing the opportunity of a visit to the two chief cities of that country when it was offered to them. The photographs and impressions we brought back with us, and which will be found in the following pages, make no claim to be more than fragmentary records and need a historical description to link them together. It is not our purpose to present one of the books of photographs which are customary nowadays, for the illustrated magazines and Cartier-Bresson's brilliant reportages have already familiarized the public with lively views of crowded Moscow streets. The few photographs of passers-by to be found here were taken from a halted car, or while we waited outside our hotel, because we thought them typical everyday scenes and snatched them without waiting for the rare appearance of a priest, a picturesque Turkoman or a pretty girl. Our attention was kept chiefly for unique monuments such as the Kremlin, of which hardly any modern photographs have as yet been published.

THE REALITY

Even with the most rapid form of transport the journey to Moscow makes one keenly conscious of the distance that separates that city from our middle-European or Western homes. The flight from Zürich to Moscow is longer than from Zürich to Casablanca. From Berlin or Prague the plane flies eastward for hour upon hour, crossing the whole of Poland and continuing its way above huge forests, marshes, fields thinly scattered with villages and cut through now and then by a thread of road or railway. One wonders if Napoleon and Hitler would have ventured to march eastwards if they could first have taken such a flight as this and realized how much toil and loneliness an advance into that far-stretched land would entail.

The local clocks are two hours ahead of our Western time when lights at last shine up over a wide area, piercing the midnight darkness, and we circle down to the long, broad landing-strip of Moscow airport with its red and green lamps.

Before we are well out of the plane we find ourselves surrounded and welcomed in the darkness by unknown figures. We do not have to undergo Customs inspection. This is our first taste of Russian hospitality —or should I call it shrewd propaganda? In my opinion it is a mistake to discount either; in Moscow one cannot draw any exact dividing-line between Russian spontaneity and Communist purpose.

We drive along a straight road through a dark, uninhabited stretch of country. Ahead of us towers a strange pyramid, outlined in red lights, which resembles a fairy-tale palace or a Hindu temple; it is the huge new University building. Suddenly, leaving the open country, we are driving between the ten-storey blocks of flats of a new suburb, with cranes pointing up into the night sky in all directions from the roofs of half-finished buildings. On we go, into the city with its wide avenues, till red stars twinkling at the peaks of two turrets show us that we have reached the Kremlin, the legendary medieval fortress of the Tsars.

There are still a few people in the streets as we enter the big Hotel Moskva in the Okhotny Riad. At this time of night the empty, dimly lit vestibule looks as inhospitable as a station booking-hall. Not until we emerge from the lift on the eighth floor do we have any sense of cheer. Here there is a lady in charge of the telephone and the keys, and heavy leather-covered armchairs stand about the corridor. My room is equipped in the style of a first-class hotel in 1914; silk bedspread, ruched silk shade on the bedside lamp, massive inkstand and blotter on the writing-table, all contributed to an impression of bourgeois comfort which is completed by a sofa and a round table bearing a plush cloth and a water carafe. A small radio set and a shower cabin are the only reminders of the fact that time has not stood still for the past fifty years. Drawing back the heavy curtains, I find myself looking straight across the street at the windows of the massive building in which the Soviet Cabinet holds its meetings. A guidebook published in Moscow begins with these jubilant words:

'Moscow! What joyful ideas and bright hopes are associated in millions of minds with the name of that city, the cradle of the Russian State, the capital of the world's first great Socialist power. . . . The heart of the Soviet Union beats here. Everything recalls the glorious past of this nation, everything bears witness to its inexhaustible might and vigour.'

They are really pilgrims, the crowds that visit this new Mecca, determined beforehand to find everything magnificent in this best of all possible worlds. Banners blowing in the breeze, they march across the Red Square; they devour statistics with as much relish as caviare, and every storey added to the huge assembly of stone and concrete, machines and ornamentation, is for them one more proof of the superiority of the régime. Many a worthy Western European too, following in the footsteps of the Red Dean of Canterbury, is enraptured by the attention shown to him, the flowers, the nursery schools, the Houses of Culture where workers go in groups for health treatments and intellectual edification, the homes for artists and the toasts drunk to Peace.

At the other extreme stand the die-hards who regard as treachery even the attempt to come to know one's opponents and measure their strength. They will give no credit for impartial judgment even to the least prejudiced visitor to Moscow, since his going there at all betokens, in their eyes, a victory for Soviet propaganda. They proved long ago that the system was quite unworkable, and are convinced that the foreigner in Russia is simply treated to a display of Potemkin villages, never being allowed to see what he wants.

It is largely owing to these preconceived ideas that a visit to Moscow is so particularly adventurous, and they make it our duty to describe clearly our own attitude on this occasion.

If 'what we want to see' consists of the secret police files, the cells where prisoners are taken for interrogation, and the plans for world conquest drawn up by those in power, if we are in search of a definite answer to the dread question of mankind's future fate, then we shall naturally be disappointed by a visit to Moscow. But if we will rest content with what can be seen in the ordinary way by a traveller in Rome, Paris or Washington, we shall be likely to profit considerably by a visit to the two chief cities of Russia. I was fortunate in making my own journey after the one-time ban on photography had been lifted, so that I could wander about without the slightest opposition and take photographs (even with a tripod) of any buildings except bridges, railway stations, factories and military installations.

In Moscow—quite apart from the fact that it is the headquarters of world Communism and of a sociological experiment whose implications cannot even yet be assessed—we are plunged into a vast, strange world with its own unfamiliar customs, history and destiny.

Before the first world war, when the European nations were hardly conscious of the frontiers dividing them, Russia was the only country for which a passport was required and a secret police force was already active there. A few years after the completion of the Trans-Siberian Railway—the culminating feat of one of Europe's most tremendous colonial operations—my parents crossed Russia on their way home from Japan; and during the pause they made in Moscow they felt further from their own country than ever before. They not only attended a performance of the famous Ballet and an impressive service in the Church of the Redeemer; they also visited the district where Maxim Gorki found the material for his *Lower Depths*, and my mother noted in her diary: 'Never have I seen anything to compare with the drunken, depraved creatures that lay about there in broad daylight. Not a hand was held out to us; we were followed by dull, brutish or resentful stares. Nowhere on our journey have we felt so conscious of social contrasts as here in Russia. Appalling poverty, flaunting wealth, beggar-women with little children whose hunger can be read in their eyes, and close at hand, ladies with huge, ostrich-plumed hats, loaded with jewels and reeking of scent; nowhere in the world have I seen vice so insolently decked out and displayed. . . . The effect of all this on us may have been intensified by our coming straight from Japan, where there is no such

13

terrible contrast between wealth and poverty.' Soon after this came war and revolution, and the Tsars' OCHRANA was almost immediately superseded by the no less redoubtable CHEKA set up by Lenin, no chance being given for the development of what the rest of Europe calls democracy.

Last but not least, the visitor to Moscow comes into contact with that most incalculable and fascinating phenomenon—the Russian human being. We know him from the great writers of the nineteenth century, and though the stronghold of Commissars and Stakhanovites is unlikely to yield us a glimpse of Oblomov, Fedja or Aliosha, their blood still runs in the veins of those who inhabit this enormous city with its façade of rigid planning and menacing capabilities.

THE THIRD ROME

It is not inappropriate that those books of mine on Rome and Byzantium which have already appeared in this series should be followed by one on the city often described by its inhabitants as the second Byzantium and the third Rome. If you count them properly, Moscow has its seven hills;

14

Ivan III

while it was from Constantinople that the Muscovites took Christianity
in its Greek Orthodox form, together with the Cyrillic script, a certain
style of architecture and writing, and the absolute authority claimed by
the autocrats who ruled in Moscow.

In 1453 the last Byzantine Emperor fell in the defence of his city. His
brother and heir-presumptive, Thomas Palaeologus, fled to Rome,
and his beautiful and intelligent daughter Zoe was brought up there.
The Great Prince of Muscovy, Ivan III, of the race of Rurik, had lost
his first wife, Maria of Tver; he sent an embassy to Rome, headed by the

Italian Master of his Mint, Giovanni Battista Volpe, to ask for Zoe's hand. Pope Paul II approved the union, in the hope that the princess, who had been brought up as a Catholic, would convert the newly arisen Eastern empire to the faith and culture of Rome. As early as 1437 the Metropolitan of Moscow, Isidore, together with the Patriarch of Constantinople, had attended the Council of Florence, whose purpose was to bring about the 'Reunions of the Church', which was sponsored by the Palaeologues and amounted, in practice, to recognition of papal supremacy; but they had failed to impose their decisions in the East.

On taking up her new station in life, Zoe changed her name to Sophia; and though Italian architects, artists and engineers were increasingly employed in Moscow, the princess's Palaeologus heredity gained the upper hand of her Roman education. The majority of priests and scholars belonged to the Greek confession; Ivan based his court ceremonial on that of Byzantium; he was the first Russian Prince to take the title of Gossudar (instead of the earlier and more modest Gospodin)

PLATE 1. Moscow. The south-east end of the Red Square, where the ground slopes down towards the Moskva River, is bounded, with dramatic effect, by one of the supreme works of Russian architecture—the Cathedral of St Basil (Vassily Blashenny). This was built by the architects Barma and Postnik, in 1554–60, during the reign of Ivan the Terrible, who chose this way of commemorating the capture of Kazan. The ground-plan is in the form of a cross; over the point of intersection rises the tent-shaped roof of the main church, the Pokrovski Cathedral; the end of each arm is crowned by an onion-shaped dome; between, rise four smaller domed turrets; these domes are all of different shapes, hence the fantastic, asymmetrical effect of the whole building. During the restoration work in 1954, the original colour-scheme was revived.

Outside the cathedral stands the monument to Minin and Pojarsky, leaders of the national uprising against the Poles in 1612; the bronze statue, by Ivan Martos, was erected in 1818 in front of the arcade of shops at one side of the Red Square, and moved to its present position when the Soviet Government made certain alterations there.

and 'Tsar of all Russia'; and he adopted as his emblem the two-headed eagle of the Byzantine Emperors.

Under Ivan III the rivalry of the Russian princely houses was at last concluded, to the advantage of Moscow; he extended the lands he had inherited to about four times their original area, and shook off the suzerainty of the Mongol 'Golden Horde'. Like many of his successors, the first Tsar of Russia was capable of cruelty and of passionate rage, usually vented on the traditionally privileged Boyars and thus adding to his popularity with the common people; after such outbursts he would revert to Christian humility and contrition. He disliked war and preferred to achieve his aims by devious diplomatic means.

Ivan made magnificent additions to his residence, the former royal stronghold of the Kremlin*. Foremost among the Italians invited to Moscow by his emissaries was Fioravante of Bologna, nicknamed 'Aristotle' owing to his versatility as artist, engineer and military expert, which resembled that of Leonardo. After him came the Milanese architects Solario and Alevisio, and others. They took the castles of Northern Italy as models for the fortresses they erected, but in building churches they brought their new methods of construction to bear on the traditional Russian style. The local master-builders apparently lacked the skill to carry out unaided the ambitious projects required to satisfy the ruler's new consciousness of power, and until the nineteenth century

* A new description of the Kremlin, its history, architecture and art treasures, is given by Arthur Voyce in his book, *The Moscow Kremlin* (University of California, 1954, and Thames & Hudson, London, 1955).

PLATE 2. The Cathedral of St Basil from the west. It is said that on the completion of the building Ivan IV (the Terrible) expressed the greatest delight, congratulating the architects on their original and masterly creation—and immediately had their eyes put out, so that they should produce no other work of equal splendour.

the majority of the most important buildings in Moscow and its rival St Petersburg were constructed by architects from the West. The successors of Ivan III tried to stem the Italian influence, probably owing to mistrust of the Pope's designs; and an increasing share of the work fell to German, English and Dutch craftsmen.

THE EARLY DAYS OF MOSCOW

The town chosen by Ivan as the nucleus of his State is mentioned for the first time in 1147, as the site of the church of Spas na boru—the Redeemer in the Forest. We are told that in 1156 the place was surrounded by a palisade of tree-trunks; and in 1237 an attack by Tartars ended in the first of the great conflagrations that recur throughout the history of Moscow. The place gained its first significance in 1263, when Daniel, the youngest son of Alexander Nevsky, established himself there as an independent princeling; and its excellent defensive possibilities attracted increasing numbers of those who were seeking refuge from the Tartars. A modest trade in local produce such as honey, wax, hemp and grain

The seal of Ivan III, with St George and the two-headed eagle.

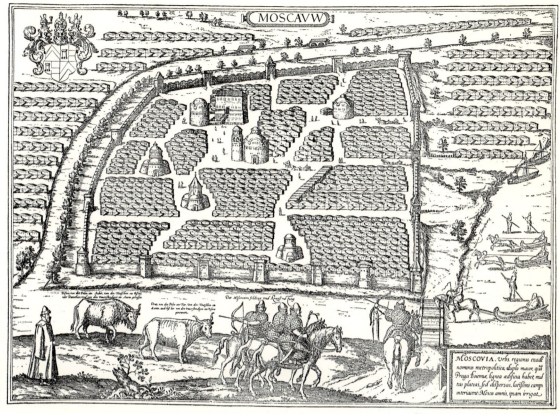

Moscow and the Kremlin in the first half of the sixteenth century.   After Herberstein

gradually developed. Ivan I (1328–40), whose inordinate covetous-
ness won him the nickname of 'money-bag', received from the Mongol
Khan the title of Great Prince and the right to levy the Tartar tribute
from all Russian princes. In the Kremlin, now mentioned in the
chronicles for the first time, he built two cathedrals; and Moscow's
fame grew so great in his day that the Metropolitan, whose first seat had
been Kiev and who had moved to Vladimir in 1299, now settled there,
accompanied by the other leaders of the Russian Church. Many holders
of the greatest ecclesiastical offices were men of strong character who

played a decisive part at crucial moments of the country's history; here, again, there is a resemblance to Constantinople, with the relationship between its Patriarch and Emperor; and the day was bound to come, as it did in 1589, when the Metropolitan of Moscow laid claim to the rank of Patriarch, the highest dignity the Orthodox Church could offer.

IVAN THE TERRIBLE AND THE WEST

Zoe, the Byzantine princess, took steps to ensure the succession for her posterity, in preference to the son of Ivan III's first marriage; she once informed the Polish Ambassador that the new Tsar's family tree could be traced back to the Emperor Augustus. Her grandson, Ivan IV (1533–84), known to history as Ivan the Terrible, energetically pursued the work begun by his grandfather, whose rage and cruelty he even exceeded. During a dispute he struck dead his own son and heir; and on his orders the Metropolitan Philip, who had ventured to reprove his terrorist methods, was driven out of the cathedral, deported and finally strangled. After which the unbridled tyrant showed deep remorse and piety and abstained from political executions during the last eight years of his reign.

Ivan made tremendous efforts to lead his country out of its primitive condition, isolation and medieval lethargy; in 1550 he convened a kind of parliament of dignitaries, known as the Semskii Sobor, and in the following year a Council of Russian ecclesiastics met in Moscow to introduce reforms. The bounds of the Empire were further extended; the conquest of Kazan and Astrakhan opened roads to the East, and unlimited prospects thus offered themselves to Moscow, the focal point of the trade routes that led in all directions through the Empire and to the Eastern and Western lands beyond its frontiers. But the Tsar's vast domains had a total population of hardly five million—no more than

The Ouspiensky
Cathedral in the
seventeenth century.
After Olearius

that of present-day Moscow—and the diplomat Freiherr von Herberstein
reported the people to be 'of such a nature that they delight more in
slavery than in freedom'. The state of the handicrafts is described by
another Austrian visitor, Prince von Buchau: 'Only in the capital are
more or less skilful artificers to be found, and most of them are Germans.
In other places hardly a craftsman exists, except tailors and shoemakers.'

Hans Slitte, from Goslar, who arrived in Moscow in 1547, was sent to
Germany by Ivan the Terrible to bring back technicians, craftsmen,

23

MOSCVA
Des grossen Jaars, Residentz
Stadt in Rußlandt

D

Plan of Moscow in the
seventeenth century.
After Olearius

artists and scholars; but on his return journey with 123 recruits, he was thrown into prison at Lübeck and kept there for eighteen months. The Hansa towns, the Teutonic Knights in Livonia, the Lithuanians, Poles and Swedes were agreed in their determination to prevent their Eastern neighbour from trading freely across the Baltic; the role of Russia should be to pay high prices for consumer and luxury goods and to deliver her cheap natural products in exchange. Among the most eagerly sought of these products, especially after the opening up of Siberia, were sables and other valuable furs. Fresh impetus was also given to trade by the enforced removal to Moscow of a number of rich merchants from Novgorod. Ivan was unsuccessful, however, in breaking through the Baltic blockade; this increased the eagerness with which he grasped the opportunity of establishing trade relations with the enterprising English. In January 1553 Captain Richard Chancelour brought his ship round the North Cape into the mouth of the Dvina, whence he made his way by sledge to Moscow; he was granted an audience by the Tsar, who promised to allow freedom of trade to English merchants; whereupon the *Russia Company* was founded in London in 1554 with a State monopoly. In the following year Chancelour returned to Moscow as ambassador of the King of England. The English opened counting-houses, English coins were accepted currency in Moscow, and the Russia Company opened successful new trade routes, especially towards Persia. Russian mistrust soon undermined the relationship, it is true, and it required all the patient diplomacy of men like Dr Giles Fletcher (who wrote a most informative book on Russia), not to mention the defeat of the Spanish Armada, to re-establish the priority of English rights over Spanish ambitions in the reign of Boris Godunov. English merchantmen were given a monopoly of trade on the Volga, and as a special favour, were exempted from torture as a means of punishment.

Among the disasters by which Moscow was afflicted, one of the most terrible was the Krim-Tartar invasion of 1571. Ivan, fully occupied in fighting the Poles and Lithuanians, made no attempt to defend the city.

The inhabitants, seeking refuge in the Kremlin, found its gates closed against them and perished by thousands in the sea of flames that engulfed their wooden huts. The population is said to have been reduced from 200,000 to 30,000. Despite setbacks of this kind, Moscow, as the focal point of a growing and highly centralized empire, steadily developed into one of the most populous cities in Europe. New districts sprang up around the Kremlin, including the Kitai Gorod (Chinatown) where the tradespeople and craftsmen lived within their own town wall, Zagorodie the 'settlement outside the city', and Zarechie, the 'settlement across the river', on the southern bank of the Moskva. Warehouses for wholesale trade were erected; the individual crafts were allotted their own special streets, and lively, colourful markets were held in the public squares, the largest of them in the Red Square. In 1553 the first book was printed in Moscow.

'THE TIME OF TROUBLES' AND THE FIRST ROMANOV

During the reign of Ivan the Terrible's childish and pious successor, Feodor, the State sank into a period of domestic wrangling for power. A Romanov came to the fore for the first time, as the young Tsar's guardian; but the hour of that dynasty had not yet struck. His place as protector was taken over by Boris Godunov, who himself accepted the crown after Feodor's death. Two of Russia's greatest artists, the poet Pushkin and the composer Mussorgsky, have related the story of Godunov, whose brief reign was marked by one of the most destructive fires and by a terrible famine. When, in 1605, Boris died of a burst blood-vessel, the false Demetrius, a putative son of Ivan IV, was approaching the city at the head of a Polish army. During these years of bewilderment the successive appearances of the fickle populace in the Red Square would have been a worthy subject for Shakespeare: they clamoured their joy at the coronation of the new Pretender—a bristle-haired man with a wart on his face and arms of unequal length—but only a year later they assembled to jeer at his dead body, beside which lay a bagpipe and a flute. Threatened by an uprising, he had tried to escape through a window of his palace in the Kremlin. Thereupon the people flocked together again to offer enthusiastic greeting to the new Tsar, Vassili Schuiskii, chosen by the Boyars; but by the summer of 1610 the Red Square was again resounding with the curses levelled at the incompetent ruler because a Polish army was approaching and the city was also threatened by a troop of rebels under the leadership of a second false Demetrius. A national uprising, in which the Church played a decisive part, finally drove out the Poles, who had occupied the capital. In January 1613 the Semskii Sobor, an assembly of 700 patriots, met to elect as the new Tsar a sixteen-year-old boy, Michael Romanov, whose family was to rule Russia for the next three hundred years.

Under the earliest Romanovs, Russia relied more than ever, for assistance in establishing itself as a civilizing element and a factor in world politics, upon the knowledge, skill and foreign connections of the Western Europeans who had settled in Moscow. A suburban district was allotted as their residence; for a time they were allowed to live in the city itself, but this soon revived the mistrust of the local people. Foreigners belonging to the Orthodox Church had separate quarters, the suburb of Basmanovka. The higher living standards and more cultivated manners of the Western Europeans formed a notable contrast to the ways of the Russian community, which were still extremely primitive. Their comfortable stone-built houses, the elegant clothes that allowed them such freedom of movement, and the artistic quality of their entertainments, had an infectious attraction for the Kremlin and the aristocracy. The Tsar had European musicians to play at his banquets, and on October 17, 1672, the first theatrical performance was presented, by members of the German School; the mild-mannered Tsar Alexis himself sat through the ten hours of *Esther*, a tragi-comedy.

Moscow. A residential district in the seventeenth century.   After Olearius

THE FOUNDING OF ST PETERSBURG

Despite the encouragement given to the Western foreigners by its rulers, the Russian Empire, while expanding further and further to the east as the power of the Mongols waned, was still denied access to the Baltic ports and the opportunity of free competition with the modern national States. The dynamic personality of Peter the Great (1689–1725) was needed to make a final breach in the westward barrier.

After the death of his half-brother Feodor in 1682, Peter was called to the throne by the council of Boyars and the Patriarch. But Sophia, his ambitious half-sister, secured the regency with the help of the 'Strelitz' who, beginning as Ivan IV's bodyguard, had developed into an arrogant clique, and the ten-year-old Tsarevitch was forced to look on at the slaughter of those who supported his mother Natalia. A frantic hunt for 'traitors' began; many were killed on the steps of the Kremlin palace itself, others were dragged to public places and handed over to the bloodthirsty and carefully engineered 'justice of the people'. The instigators of the massacre erected a memorial in the Red Square in the attempt to justify themselves to posterity; but sixteen years later, Peter took an equally ferocious revenge when he suppressed the revolt by which the Strelitz had striven to oppose his reforms.

In the meantime the young Tsar had grown to manhood far from all State concerns, living among the peasants in the country round Moscow. Here he studied many crafts, of which the soldier's roused his most passionate interest, though he also turned to shipbuilding and navigation with enthusiasm. On coming of age he chose as his mentors a Scottish military engineer, Patrick Gordon, and an adroit Genevan, François Lefort, whom he made an admiral. After his first campaign, which led to the capture of Azov, he pressed forward the construction of a navy, sent young Russians to Europe for training, and finally set out himself to investigate the superior qualities of the more advanced countries. He caroused with foreign sailors at Libau, had himself

PLATE 3. Moscow. Below the west wall of the Kremlin lies a public park, the Alexander Gardens. In the background rises the tower above the Troitski (Trinity) Gate, which, with the exception of the Spasski Gate, is the highest of the Kremlin's twenty gate-towers. In olden times the Neglinka River flowed past here, as a further line of defence for the stronghold; but in 1817–19 this was covered in with a brick roof, and in 1826 Beauvais laid out the Alexander Gardens above it.

initiated into the mysteries of artillery by an expert at Königsberg, worked as a carpenter and shipwright in Holland, and travelled round England for several months, chiefly in order to visit factories and work-shops. Back in the Kremlin, he gave audience to the dignitaries of Moscow and cut off their beards with his own hand, sparing only the Patriarch and two ancient Boyars from this drastic violation of sacrosanct custom (the shaving of beards was forbidden on pain of excommunication). On January 4, 1700, he issued a Ukase decreeing the reform of dress, which was to follow Hungarian, German or French models; shears were used when necessary to curtail the unpractical length of the Asian-style sleeves and shirt-tails, and the Tsar ordered samples of the new clothes to be hung up at the city gates. When the Patriarch Hadrian died, later in the year, Peter banned the election of a successor and subsequently trans-ferred the functions of this high office to the 'most holy and sovereign Synod'.

In May 1703, undismayed by the defeat Charles XII had inflicted on him two and a half years previously at Narva, Peter set to work to secure for himself the Baltic port that nature and Sweden had hitherto denied him. Having captured the Swedish fortress of Nöteborg, at the point

PLATE 4. Moscow. View from the Great Stone Bridge (Bolshoi Kamenny Most) over the Moskva River towards the Kremlin. *Left*, the south-west corner tower of the Kremlin wall, known as the Water Tower (Vodasvodnaia bashnia) because of the pumping apparatus it houses; this tower was built in 1488, restored in 1805, demolished at the order of Napoleon in 1812, and rebuilt in 1817. *Centre*, the Great Kremlin Palace (Bolshoi Kremlensky Dvorets), built for Nicholas I in 1838–49, by the architect K. A. Thon, on the site of an earlier palace and various other buildings. *Right*, the Kremlin Cathedral, whose belfry, the Tower of Ivan the Great, rises high above the surrounding roofs.

where the Neva flows out of Lake Ladoga, together with Nyenschanz at the mouth of the Neva, he founded a church dedicated to the Apostles Peter and Paul on the little island of Saiatschie, where the Neva divides into the two main streams of its delta. With his own hands he dug a cavity in the foundations to hold a golden box containing relics of St Andrew the Apostle, and two days later he ordered a fortress to be built close by, on what was still regarded as Swedish territory. The marshy land, continually in danger of flooding, could hardly have seemed less promising as the site of a town; but it offered the features essential to a harbour on the Gulf of Finland, and the river linked it with the system of communications in Russia itself.

If ever a city was created out of nothing by the determination and untiring efforts of a single individual, it was this inhospitable spot, dedicated with full ecclesiastical pomp by the Metropolitan of Novgorod under the name of 'Sankt Piter Burch'.

An army of workers was summoned. Volunteers, lured by all kinds of promises, soldiers, prisoners of war; even the prisons opened their doors and thousands of criminals came to toil on the Neva. Masons

PLATE 5. Leningrad. View from the quay beside the monument to Peter the Great, towards the Vassilievsky Ostrov (Island), lying between the two arms of the Neva, showing the Museum and Academy buildings on the University bank. *Left*, the Academy of Science, built by Guarenghi in 1784–7, during the reign of Catherine II; Peter the Great had made plans for its foundation, which were carried out by Catherine I in 1725; it has been known since 1925 as the Academy of the Soviet Union. The neighbouring building, with its central tower, was constructed in 1718–25 by Mattarnuovi to house Peter the Great's collections of curiosities and works of art, and to serve as an observatory; it is now the Soviet Union Central Museum of Anthropology and Ethnography. *Right*, the projecting southern tip of the Island, the Strelka, with one of the rostral columns.

М.А.КОДЛО.

were forced into the work by a decree which permitted only wooden houses to be built elsewhere in the empire for a number of years. Epidemics took heavy toll of the ill-lodged and underfed labourers. Peter built himself a simple wooden house in the middle of the future city and applied his iron will to overcoming all obstacles. Shipyards and Admiralty offices were his foremost concern, but his plans already showed what were to become the chief features of the city, such as the later celebrated Nevski Prospect, cut through the forest from the Neva to a point where a monastery was erected to receive the bones of Alexander Nevsky, who had defeated the Swedes in 1240. In November 1703 the first Dutch merchantmen sailed into the new harbour, to be greeted with jubilation.

The Tsar's most powerful enemy, Charles XII of Sweden, watched all this activity derisively from a distance, confident that he could easily dismiss the challenge. But he was utterly routed at Poltava on July 8, 1709, which justified Peter's exultant declaration, 'Now, with God's help, Petersburg is truly established!'

'Pétersbourg est la fenêtre par laquelle la Russie regarde l'Europe,' said Francesco Algarotti, the guest of Frederick the Great at Sans Souci, in a phrase which became celebrated in history.

Ten years after the foundation of the city Peter took his second decisive step by transferring the Government and the entire administration there. His intention was to set a permanent course for the future

PLATE 6. The founder of St Petersburg—Peter I Alexeievich, born 1672, proclaimed Tsar in 1682, died February 8, 1725. The head, modelled in clay by the French artist Marie Collot, for the monument to Peter the Great designed by her uncle and teacher, E. M. Falconnet. Russian Museum, Leningrad.

development of his people, and to remove his collaborators from the influence of Moscow, with its unyielding traditions, its hostility to foreigners, its intrigues and its reluctance to accept any kind of innovation. In 1717 the Tsar visited Paris, returning with a host of new projects suggested by the numerous palaces and enterprises of various kinds that he had inspected there. The Peace of Nystad, by which Russia's position on the Baltic was secured in 1721, was celebrated with full baroque splendour, which included a public masquerade that continued for several days. The Tsar drank and sang with the best, and danced boisterously on tables. He now claimed the title of 'Emperor' and was recognized as such by the other powers. Even his contemporaries referred to him as 'the Great'. He died on February 8, 1725, in his fifty-third year, as the result of a chill caught in going to the rescue of a stranded boat.

PLATES 7–8. Leningrad.

PLATE 7. The monument to Peter the Great, beside the Neva. In 1766 Etienne Maurice Falconnet, a member of the Paris Academy, was commissioned by Catherine II to design a statue of the Emperor. The plaster cast was completed in 1779; the following year, with the eager approval of the Empress, the 1,600-ton block of granite on which the bronze statue was to stand was transported from the village of Lasht to Petersburg, a distance of some seven miles; and the statue was ceremoniously unveiled in August 1782. The pedestal bears the inscription: 'To Peter the First—Catherine the Second', in Latin on one side and Russian on the other.

PLATE 8. The Winter Palace, now renamed the 'Palace of Art'—the official residence of the Tsars until 1917—forms a rectangle 498 feet long by 384 feet wide, and contains 700 rooms; it was built by Rastrelli in 1754–62, during the reign of the Empress Elizabeth. After the abdication of Nicholas II, Kerensky's Provisional Government established itself there; the building now houses the art treasures from the Hermitage. This view shows the Southern façade overlooking the former Castle Square, with the Admiralty in the background.

The lack of an energetic successor to the throne endangered Peter's reforms and the future of his new capital. His widow, Catherine I, continued his pro-Western policy with the help of her favourite, Menshikov. But she died after only two years in power, and reaction seemed likely to triumph under her young grandson, Peter II. Menshikov was banished and the court moved back to Moscow; many inhabitants of Petersburg showed an inclination to leave the city of their enforced residence.

After the early death of Peter II the Privy Council gave the crown to Anna Ivanovna (1730–40), a niece of Peter the Great. For the next seventy years the fate of the empire lay chiefly in the hands of women, and it was they who saved the great emperor's life's work from destruction and made Petersburg into one of the most brilliant cities of Europe.

Anna Ivanovna was succeeded by a minor, Ivan VI, whose mother, Anna Leopoldovna, acted as regent. Early one December morning, only a year after his accession, mother and son were woken from sleep in the Winter Palace by the news that Elizabeth, a daughter born to Peter the Great and the future Catherine I before their marriage, had led

PLATE 9. Leningrad. The Cathedral of St Isaac of Kiev, a masterpiece of the 'Empire' period, dominates with its gilded dome, 367 feet high, the square behind the Peter I memorial, surrounded as it is with monumental buildings. It was built in 1817–58 by the French architect Montferrand on the site of a wooden church erected by Peter I, and displays huge columns of granite and a wealth of sculpture. Immense foundations were required to sustain the vast building on the marshy ground.

a successful revolt during the night and was now the ruler of Russia. Elizabeth I (1741–62) enjoyed to the full the effect of her charms on the male sex; but despite a rudimentary education her political genius was so marked that Frederick the Great dreaded her unrelenting opposition and was much relieved by the news of her death. Her policy was strongly nationalist, but she did not close the country to Western cultural influences. Italian, French and German architects carried out many magnificent projects in the baroque style, such as the great new Winter Palace built by Bartolomeo Rastrelli. In literature and the theatre French influences preponderated. It was Elizabeth who founded the Petersburg Academy of Fine Art (1758) and the University of Moscow.

Elizabeth was succeeded by her nephew, Peter III, son of the Duke of Holstein-Gottorp and grandson, on his mother's side, of Peter I. He lost no opportunity of expressing his boundless admiration for Frederick II of Prussia, and made himself impossible by his contempt for everything Russian. His own wife, a princess of Anhalt-Zerbst, became leader of the malcontents and acceded to the throne, as Catherine II (1762–96). This remarkable woman set herself to preserve the Byzantine autocracy while introducing the most up-to-date of Western ideas. Her confidants were always Russians. She did not shrink from secularizing the property of the Church to raise funds for the State; she founded a wide variety of schools and institutions, sent promising subjects to be

PLATE 10. Leningrad. Main entrance to the Admiralty. This building, which stands at the centre of Petersburg, was begun by Peter I immediately after the fortress of SS. Peter and Paul had been laid out on the opposite bank of the Neva, and was considerably enlarged soon after his death; its final aspect, with the sculpture decorating its façade, dates from 1823, when the architect Sakharov worked on it for Alexander I. The groups of statuary beside the main entrance—nymphs supporting the globe—are by Shchedrin.

trained in foreign countries, drafted a new code of laws and undertook single-handed the administration of the Empire. She corresponded with Voltaire and was visited by Diderot, whom she had generously helped when he was in financial difficulties. The quays bordering the Neva and a number of new palaces were built, bringing Petersburg close to the majestic perfection it shows today; and the erection of the celebrated equestrian statue of Peter the Great with its brief inscription, 'Petro primo Catharina secunda' bore witness to the Empress's pride at having continued the work of her great predecessor.

Under the six emperors who followed one another on the throne during the nineteenth century, Russia continued as a two-headed Janus, sometimes taking on the aspect of a European power like any other, sometimes appearing as a sinister, alien, oriental autocracy. Bold reforms, opening wide the door to the West in an attempt to keep up with the frenzied pace of European technological and economic progress, alternated with harsh police measures reflecting deep-seated mistrust of everything new and foreign. But the Tsar as sole ruler of all the Russians never allowed his position as anointed autocrat to be seriously questioned, and to the very last the two-headed eagle topped every tower and adorned the façade of every palace, as a symbol of the Byzantine heritage.

Paul I (1796–1801) prohibited foreign travel and established a strict literary censorship. Alexander I (1801–25) began his reign as an

PLATE 11. Leningrad. The Admiralty, from the 'Workers' Garden', formerly the Alexander Gardens. The tower which rises to a height of 230 feet in the centre of the 1377 feet façade (whose length is, in fact, 2559 feet if the two wings are included) was built in 1734–5.

enthusiastic exponent of Rousseau's ideas, derived from his Genevan tutor, Laharpe; he gave a free hand to the eager reformer, Speransky, but suddenly dismissed him from office in 1812. Nicholas I (1825–55) reimposed a strict censorship, reduced dealings with foreign countries to the unavoidable minimum, introduced military drill into the high schools and gave preference to political reliability in the appointment of officials and university professors. Alexander II (1855–81), educated by the poet Schukovsky, gained the title of Liberator by abolishing serfdom in 1861; he was killed by an anarchist's bomb when driving back from a military review. Alexander III (1881–94) reverted to political and religious intolerance and favoured the pan-Slav movement. During the reign of the last tragic figure, Nicholas II, the divergent tendencies at last came into conflict and under the pressure of events with which even a stronger personality than his could hardly have dealt successfully. Meanwhile, however, despite all its crises, the little princedom of Muscovy had expanded, almost unnoticed by the rest of Europe, into a colonial power of the first order, whose territories extended from the Baltic to the Sea of Japan.

NAPOLEON IN THE KREMLIN

During the rapid growth of St Petersburg, whose population exceeded 200,000 in Catherine's reign and had risen to a million by the end of the nineteenth century, Moscow successfully retained its rank as the elder of the two capitals, the heart of the nation, the city to which every new ruler must come to be anointed and crowned in the Cathedral of the Ascension, within the Kremlin walls.

Moscow was Napoleon's aim when he undertook his Russian campaign in 1812. Alexander I summoned the aristocrats and the merchants to the Kremlin, where he proclaimed the need for them, and the nation as a whole, to rise in defence of their fatherland. On September 2 the French advance-guard entered Moscow, and from the Sparrow Hills (now the Lenin Hills, where the new University stands) Napoleon glimpsed the towers and gleaming domes of his goal. But the Tsar, the Governor Rostoptschin and the vast majority of the population of about 240,000 had left the city, and when, on the following day, the French Emperor entered the Kremlin, flames whose origin was never fully established were already rising from the deserted market-places and courtyards. By September 6, when heavy rain put an end to the con-flagration, between 80 and 90 per cent of the houses were destroyed. On September 24 a snowstorm heralded the onset of winter, and on October 7 Napoleon and his army began their retreat.

With increased self-confidence Moscow set about its rebuilding. Industrialization soon began here, as at St Petersburg. Fresh stimulus was provided by the railways; Moscow developed into the junction of eleven lines, and by the beginning of the twentieth century between 15 and 20 per cent of all goods carried by the railways in European Russia was loaded or unloaded there. The population, while remaining slightly less than that of the other capital, increased to 364,000 by 1864, to 768,000 by 1882, to 1,092,000 by 1902, and had almost reached 2,000,000 when the 1914 war broke out.

THE OLD AND THE NEW CAPITAL

It was during the nineteenth century that the Russian middle class, its development favoured by the parallel growth and perpetual inter-change of ideas of the rival capitals, emerged from the tutelage of enlightened despotism and gave worthy expression in art to the dormant creative energies of a great nation.

Towards 1830 the young Nicolai Gogol, newly appointed to a post in the Civil Service at St Petersburg, described the points of difference between his new place of residence and his former home:

'. . . A really extraordinary idea, to put the capital of Russia at the world's end!. . . As though Moscow were not cold enough, we had to be given Petersburg! And the wild wasteland that separates Mother Moscow from her little son! The air is heavy with fog and the wan, grey-green earth bears nothing except charred tree-stumps, pines and hummocks of grass. . . . The only consolation is the dead-straight road along which the singing, rattling troikas carry one at lightning speed. And what a difference, what a tremendous difference, between the two towns!

'Even today Moscow is still the bearded Russian, while Petersburg is already a polished European. Old Moscow spreads itself out and lolls at ease, whereas Petersburg, the fop, stands at attention, fingers pressed against trouser-seams! Mirrors surround it on all sides—the Neva, the Gulf of Finland, the canals. Ample opportunity for self-admiration. . . . Petersburg is in perpetual motion, from cellar to attic; at midnight it

PLATES 12–16. Leningrad.

PLATE 12. View from the Strelka towards the Fortress of Peter and Paul. In the middle is the church of the fortress, with its tower 393 feet high.

PLATE 13. Opposite the south front of the Winter Palace is the building formerly occupied by the General Staff of the Army; it was built in 1819–47 by Rossi, the architect responsible for the additions made to Petersburg during that period.

PLATE 14. The building erected for the Senate (the supreme court of justice in Tsarist times) and the connected premises of the Holy Synod were constructed together by Rossi in 1829–35.

PLATE 15. The monument to the Emperor Nicholas I (1825–55); designed by Klodt in 1859.

PLATE 16. The main entrance of the Museum, built in 1840–52 by Klenze to house the imperial collection from the Hermitage; it is decorated with ten caryatids carved in grey granite.

begins to bake the French rolls which will be devoured next morning by all the different nationalities that make up its population, and one or another of its yellow eyes is always blinking through the darkness. Whereas Moscow snores all night and sets out at daybreak, crossing itself and bowing to all four points of the compass, to eat its modest breakfast in the market.

'Petersburg is a gentleman of scrupulous deportment, a true German, reckoning every penny and carefully weighing his purse before sending out invitations for a *soirée*; but Moscow is a *grand seigneur*, pursuing a pleasure, once begun, to the point of exhaustion, with little care for the fact that his funds have long given out. . . .

'The Moscow newspapers speak of Kant, Schelling and so forth; the Petersburg papers talk of nothing but the public and solvency. In Moscow the papers keep pace with the times, but are apt to be late in appearing; in Petersburg the papers are entirely behind the times, but appear punctually at the appointed hour. In Moscow a writer can whistle for his money, in Petersburg he earns some.

'Moscow, swathed in bearskins, drives in carriages, usually on the way to a meal; Petersburg, hands in mackintosh pockets, rushes on foot to

PLATES 17–18. Leningrad.

PLATE 17. Looking across the Neva towards the Strelka—the eastern point of the Vassilievsky Island. The Exchange building, with its classical Doric colonnade, was begun in 1784 and completed by Thomas de Thomon in 1810–16; in front of it stand two rostral columns as landmarks for ships.

PLATE 18. The Smolny Institute, which stands next to the convent of the same name, was founded by Catherine II for the purpose of educating girls from noble families according to the most advanced principles of the period. The classical building was erected by Guarenghi in 1806–8. The first All-Russian Soviet Congress met here in 1917 and it was from here that the Revolutionary War Committee, headed by Lenin, launched the October Revolution.

the Stock Exchange or "to go on duty". The whole of Russia glides in sledges to Moscow in the winter, to buy and sell; the peasants trudge to Petersburg in the summer, to find work. Moscow is a huge warehouse, Petersburg a brightly-lit shop. Moscow is indispensable to Russia, Russia is indispensable to Petersburg. . . .

'Petersburg is fond of laughing at Moscow for its bad taste and awkwardness, but Moscow retorts scornfully that Petersburg cannot even speak Russian.'

THE GOLDEN AGE OF RUSSIAN CIVILIZATION

Gogol was not the only Russian writer to divide his life between the two cities; it was characteristic of Russians in general to spend some time gazing from the 'window onto Europe' at the latest intellectual developments and then return to the ancient centre of the land and imbibe mystical inspiration from the national spirit.

Pushkin described the superficial brilliance of Petersburg society in *Eugen Onegin* and sang the praises of its mighty founder in *The Bronze Horseman*; Grigoriev wrote poems to the melancholy beauty of its white nights; it was on the banks of the Neva that Dostoievsky, a native of Moscow, revealed to world literature the sinister atmosphere of the new

PLATE 19. Moscow, the Kremlin. Next to the Great Palace of the Kremlin, at the entrance of the Cathedral Square and facing the Archangelsky Cathedral (plate 21) stands the Blagoveschenski (Cathedral of the Annunciation), the court church of Ivan III. It was built in 1484–9, by architects from Pskov, on the site of a church erected a hundred years earlier by the Great Prince Vassily Dimitrievich, and was enlarged during the reign of Ivan IV. It is based, even more definitely than the larger Ouspiensky Cathedral, on the style of Vladimir.

intellectual proletariat; Belyi, in his novel *Petersburg* (1912), protested against the tutelage of the West. Tolstoy divided his time between Petersburg and Moscow before finally retiring to his estate at Yasnaya Polyana. Turgeniev, after his student years in Moscow and Petersburg, spent the greater part of his life abroad, and many other important writers escaped from the continual oppression of the censorship into a freer world. But Gontscharov, whose *Oblomov* so vividly depicts the Russian tendency to indolence, ended his Civil Service career as a member of the board of censors in Petersburg.

The writers of Moscow contributed no less to Russian cultural development than those of Petersburg, and the theatre was particularly prominent there. In the 1880s the lead was taken by the Mali (Little) Theatre—the equivalent of the Alexandrinsky at Petersburg—while a unique form of realism was later achieved by Stanislavsky's Art Theatre, where Tchekov's *Seagull* was presented with striking success in December 1898, shortly after being hissed at its first performance in the Court Theatre at Petersburg.

PLATE 20. Moscow, the Kremlin. Looking from the public garden on the southern slope below the fortress, towards one of the classical-style Government buildings and the Tower of the Redeemer (Spaskie Vorota). This, the tallest of the Kremlin towers (237 feet), is the main entrance to the stronghold. Until 1917 a lamp was kept perpetually burning before the picture of the Redeemer above the outer gateway, and all passers-by took off their hats to it. The tower was built in 1491 by Marco Ruffo in the style of an Italian *castello*; in 1625, during the reign of the first Romanov, an Englishman, Christopher Halloway, replaced the original battlements by a Gothic superstructure containing a set of chimes. The Tsars made their ceremonial entrance through the Spasski Gate when they came to be crowned; and on the days of great religious ceremonies the processions emerged through it on their way from the Patriarch's residence to the Cathedral of St Basil in the Red Square.

Glinka's *A Life for the Tsar*, first produced in 1836 at the Petersburg Opera House, opened a no less brilliant chapter in the musical history of Russia, which found its chief outlet in Petersburg and whose distinguished figures included the internationally celebrated pianist, Anton Rubinstein—co-founder, with Carl Schuberth, of the famous Conservatoire (1862)—his scarcely less gifted brother Nicholas, who established the corresponding institution in Moscow (1869); Tchaikovsky, who taught in the Petersburg Conservatoire for eleven years before deciding to devote himself entirely to composition; Balakirev, who in 1862 established the 'Free School of Music' where the ideas of the new Russian composers—Borodin, Mussorgsky and Rimsky-Korsakov—prevailed in opposition to the official Conservatoire.

In Moscow the classical Opera House (the Bolshoi, or 'Large' Theatre), with its gilded auditorium to hold 4,000 spectators, was rebuilt and reopened in 1856, the original building of 1824 having been destroyed by fire in 1853; and in 1860 a Petersburg circus was

PLATES 21–2. Moscow.

PLATE 21. The Kremlin. The Cathedral of Michael the Archangel (Archangelsky Sobor) was originally built of wood, in the thirteenth century. In 1333 it was rebuilt in stone, to serve as the mortuary church of the Great Princes of Moscow. In 1505 Ivan III had it entirely renovated, with incomparable magnificence, as part of the restoration of the Kremlin, for which he had brought architects from Italy: this particular task being entrusted to Alevisio Novo, a Milanese, who thus opened new prospects for Russian ecclesiastical architecture, introducing Italian renaissance features. Up to the time of Peter I all the Tsars were buried here.

PLATE 22. The Cathedral Square in the Kremlin, with the Patriarchal Palace and the Church of the Twelve Apostles. This group of buildings, dating from 1655–56, was restored in 1918–22, during which process it was relieved of later accretions and the vaulted passageways were again revealed.

transformed into the elegant Marinsky Theatre. The classical ballet of the European tradition had its last triumphs in these two houses, where Pavlova and Karsavina danced before the Tsar and his guests.

The cultural riches and brilliant ceremonial of both capitals were enhanced by the two Universities and the other colleges with their thousands of students, the learned societies, the academies of art, the museums and monuments, not forgetting the glittering trappings of the bodyguard that surrounded the sacred person of the Emperor.

ENDURING TRADITIONS

Nearly half a century has gone by since those days, a time of tremendous changes everywhere. But the visitor who comes to the two cities with this fact in mind will be less astonished by what is new than by the survival of tradition and in many cases by the pride shown in preserving

PLATE 23. Moscow, Kremlin. The Church of the Ascension (Ouspiensky Sobor), built in honour of the Ascension of the Holy Virgin, is the largest of the Kremlin churches; within its walls, with their wealth of frescoes, the Tsars were crowned by the Patriarch or by the Metropolitan of Moscow; a number of princes of the Church are buried here, and the building was the scene of many dramatic events in Russian history. The church was founded by the Metropolitan Peter in 1326, during the reign of Ivan Kalita. In 1475 Ivan III commissioned the Bolognese architect Rodolfo Fioravante, nicknamed 'Aristotle', to erect a new and more splendid building, after the pattern of the Ouspiensky Cathedral at Vladimir. Fioravante made a thorough study of the ancient monuments of Russian architecture, but introduced new methods of construction, together with certain Italian elements. A resemblance to St Mark's Cathedral in Venice testifies to the Byzantine origin of both buildings.

it. The 'glorious past of the nation' referred to in the Soviet guidebook to Moscow is displayed to us on all sides in the carefully preserved buildings dating from the days of the great Tsars; and an attachment to old-style decoration, middle-class stolidity, courtly pomp and resplendent parades has been carried over into today's bombastic demonstrations of proletarian culture. In the brightly lit theatres with their rows of boxes Prince Igor and other heroes of Russian history bestride the stage, and the thunderous applause once earned by Karsavina now goes to Ulanova. Just as in the old days, the samovar bubbles in winter on the heavily laden table to which the guest is invited, and the vodka flows as freely as before. True, the faces of those in power, glimpsed from time to time in a box at the theatre, from a distance on a grandstand or in cinema close-ups, have changed from the aristocratic features marked by their resemblance to related royal houses; the powerful peasant type now predominates—men who have made their own way to the top, sometimes from a nation whose territory lies far away in Asia. But they, like their predecessors, hold secret cabinet meetings from which they issue their Ukases and at which their whole future may be staked on a gamble. And they too have their henchmen, uniformed or civilian figures with inscrutable faces, who go about their business in streets, offices, hotels, seen or unseen but always present.

PLATES 24–5. Moscow.

PLATE 24. Façade of a two-storey patrician house.

PLATE 25. Two-storey wooden houses in the Chamovniki district—typical of the residential districts of nineteenth-century Moscow; now rare and doubtless fated before long to vanish altogether.

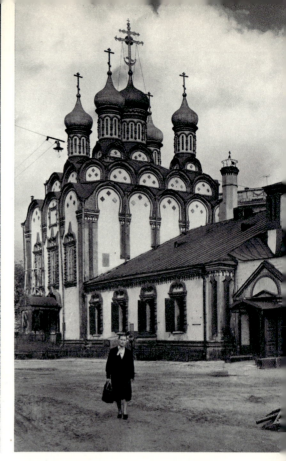

This is of course an entirely different order of things from that foreseen by Bakunin, the father of the Russian revolution, when he proclaimed in 1848 that 'In Moscow a star will rise aloft in splendour from a sea of blood and flame, to become the guiding star of salvation for all mankind!' For he said, too, 'I hate Communism because it is the negation of freedom and because humanity without freedom is inconceivable to me!' He wanted the principle of authority 'to be extirpated root and branch'; freedom through anarchy, anarchy through freedom, was the revolutionary cry that rose from the Russian soul when at last it hardened itself to oppose autocracy and uniforms. But Lenin was a realist, concerned with the new State whose dogma was to be founded no longer on the grace of God but on the infallibility of the Socialist system.

PLATES 26-9. Churches and monasteries in old Moscow.

PLATE 26. Tower in the courtyard of the Domskoi Monastery, founded in 1592 by Fyodor I after the victory over the Tartars; now an architectural museum.

PLATE 27. The church of Nicholas the Miracle-worker, in the Chamovniki district, built by local craftsmen in 1679-86.

PLATE 28. One of the churches whose domes and towers used to rise above the roofs of Moscow, but which are now hidden among massive modern buildings.

PLATE 29. Beside the ramparts of the Novodievitzi (New Virgin) Convent, the largest and richest in Moscow, founded in 1524. After the death of Tsar Fyodor (1598), his widow, Irene, entered this convent as a nun; in 1689 the Regent Sophia, elder sister of Peter I, was obliged to do the same. In 1922 the institution, with its fine buildings, was turned into a museum. Above the walls rises the slender baroque belfry, dating from the end of the seventeenth century.

In January 1905, as a result of the impression made by Japan's defeat of Russia, the first wave of revolution broke over the land. The workers in several Petersburg factories went on strike, unrest spread to the peasants, subversive ideas were rife among the middle-class intelligentsia, who were in perpetual difficulties with the censorship and constantly threatened with banishment to Siberia. On January 9 (Russian calendar), a Sunday, a vast crowd of men, women and children, carrying ikons and religious banners and led by a priest named Gapon, marched to the Winter Palace to present the Tsar with a petition bearing 135,000 signatures and imploring his 'justice and protection'. But Nicholas II had withdrawn to his summer residence, Tsarskoye Selo, and troops were lined up ready to scatter the crowd with a fusillade that left over a thousand dead on the ground. Strike after industrial strike followed this 'bloody Sunday'; the idea of an armed uprising gained more and more adherents, and in May the first 'Soviet' was organized in one factory. In October the agitation rose to fresh heights, the strike movement had by now spread almost throughout Russia, the Mensheviks launched their 'Soviet of Workers' Representatives' and a corresponding Moscow Soviet had already passed under the control of the more extreme Bolsheviks. But the storm was averted for the last time by the Tsar's October Manifesto, drawn up by Witte, with its pledge of liberal reforms. By November 20, when Lenin, the declared leader of the Bolsheviks, at last reached Petersburg from his exile in Geneva, the movement had already passed its climax. True, there was a run on the Petersburg savings-banks in December, but some of the Soviet members were arrested, the attempt at a new general strike was unsuccessful, and when the more extreme workers in Moscow broke into open revolt and erected barricades, they were overpowered by the Government troops. The liberal middle classes now turned to the Duma, a parliamentary body with merely advisory powers, in the attempt to influence State affairs. But Lenin had no thought of coming to terms with the bourgeois opposition; he was bent upon the dictatorship of the proletariat and ordered his followers to concentrate for the time being on accumulating fresh revolutionary energy. In December 1907 he fled through fog and darkness across the brittle ice of the Gulf of Finland and made his way back to his refuge in Switzerland, whence he continued to impose his will on the underground activities of the Party.

In July 1914, though the menace of strikes loomed again in the Petersburg suburbs, the Tsar's palace on the Neva showed its brilliant façade to the world once more, in honour of a visit from President Poincaré. Maurice Paléologue, one of France's most acute diplomats, then Ambassador to Russia, gives a full account in his memoirs of this social and political event. The parades and banquets were hardly over, the final toast scarcely drunk, when on July 23, with Austria's ultimatum to Serbia, war broke out in Europe. On July 29, Nicholas II signed the decree ordering general mobilization, rescinded it at the request of his cousin the Kaiser, but reissued it on the following day. On September 1, 1914, St Petersburg was renamed Petrograd, in an attempt to efface the memory of the strong German influence that had prevailed there.

Fresh unrest resulted from the unexpected duration of the war, in which the ill-prepared Russian army held out surprisingly well against the well-equipped Austrians and Germans. The cumbersome administrative machinery began to slip from the control of the Petersburg officials; there was a shortage of munitions, food supplies to the towns were irregular, sabotage was widespread in the heavy industries. When troops were called in to quell strikers, they mutinied; in Petrograd the workers' and soldiers' Soviet was vying for authority with the Duma.

On March 2 (March 15 new style), in his special train—halted at Pskov on its way from military headquarters to Tsarskoye Selo—Nicholas II signed his abdication. On the same day the new Government held its first meeting, under Prince Lvov, at the Tauride Palace.

On April 16 (April 3 old style) Lenin was given an impressive reception at the Finland Station in Petrograd. With thirty other emigrants he had travelled back from Switzerland through Germany thanks to the complicity of the German high command, which was interested in his peace propaganda.

However, when the All-Russian Soviet Congress met in Petrograd on June 16, the Bolsheviks were still in the minority as compared with the Social Revolutionary party and the Mensheviks. On July 17 the workers of the great Putilov factory attempted to seize power. Lenin harangued the crowd from the balcony of the Villa Kschessinskaya—the Communist headquarters—and demonstrators surged round the

PLATES 30–2. Moscow.

PLATES 30–1. The Great (Bolshoi) Theatre, built by Bove and Michailov in 1824, was destroyed by fire in 1853 and reconstructed in its present form, with its imposing classical façade, by Cavos in 1856. The auditorium seats 4,000. This building and the Maryinsky Theatre at Petersburg became the great strongholds of Russian opera and the world-famous Russian Ballet. Plate 31 shows a performance of Tchaikovsky's ballet, 'Swan Lake'.

PLATE 32. The Red Square, looking eastwards. In the foreground, the stands for the great parades, with in the centre the Lenin Mausoleum, erected in 1924 to the design of Shchusev—first in wood and later in stone faced with black and grey Labrador granite and red Ukrainian granite. To the right the Kremlin wall, with the Senate Tower—at the foot of which were dug the 'Brothers' graves' (Bratskie mogily) for the revolutionaries killed in October 1917—and the Gate of the Redeemer. To the left, the Red Square with the familiar outline of the Cathedral of St Basil; further left, the southern end of the arcade of shops. In the background the skyscraper apartment block on the Kotelniki quay (built in 1952).

Tauride Palace. But the uprising was suppressed; Lenin escaped imprisonment by shaving off his beard and travelling away, unrecognized, as the fireman of a railway engine; not till the end of September did he venture secretly back to Petrograd to wait for his moment. Meanwhile the eloquent Kerensky had risen from Minister of Justice to War Minister and finally to Prime Minister with dictatorial powers. He established his coalition government in the royal suite in the Winter Palace and sat himself down at Alexander II's writing-desk.

Lenin's supporters gained control of the Petrograd Soviet, and Trotsky was elected as its new Chairman. On October 24 (November 6) Kerensky announced to the 'preliminary Parliament' assembled in the Marinsky Palace that the Bolsheviks were planning an uprising, but that appropriate measures had been taken to counter this. On the afternoon of the same day, Lenin—for whom the police were searching—made his way, in a disguise complete with wig, to the former Smolny Institute, a girl's school, now the Communist headquarters. Despite the Government's precautionary measures, the *coup d'état* was completed without a hitch in the course of the following night. All key positions

PLATES 33–4. Moscow.

PLATE 33. At the corner of Okhotny Riad and Pushkin Street stands the Trade Union building, the former Club of the nobility and scene of great festivities. The house was built in 1785 by Matvei Kasakov for Field-Marshal Prince Dolgoruki. The body of Lenin lay in state in its pillared hall at the end of January 1924, before the funeral ceremony.

PLATE 34. The Ministry of Light Industry and Textiles, Kirov Street. As a result of two competitions, a design by Le Corbusier was selected in 1928, and carried out in 1929–34. The building, constructed of reinforced concrete, was planned to provide office space for 3,500 employees and was originally intended as the headquarters of the Co-operative Society. A design for the Palace of the Soviets, submitted by Le Corbusier in 1931, was rejected.

were occupied—telephone exchanges, post offices, the State Bank, the railway stations, the seat of the preliminary Parliament and the various Ministries. The provisional Government in the Winter Palace found itself isolated. Kerensky succeeded in escaping from the city by car, but was unable to raise troops from outside. On October 26 (November 8) the Winter Palace was taken by storm and the remaining Ministers had to surrender. Early on the same morning the Soviet Congress, which was meeting at the Smolny Institute, had proclaimed the establishment of the Council of People's Commissars under the presidency of Lenin, the immediate conclusion of peace, and the abolition of landed property.

The seizure of power in Moscow was delayed for a few days longer. Colonel Riabzve, the commander of the garrison, withdrew with his faithful supporters to the Kremlin, but the arrival of reinforcements for the Bolsheviks made his position hopeless and he was forced to capitulate.

The population took some time to realize what had happened. In Petrograd and Moscow alike the press, whatever its shade of opinion, had grown accustomed to expressing itself freely; and amid all the miseries of war, the coal shortage and the starvation rations, the liberal-minded middle classes had been enjoying their liberation from autocracy; drama and music had never been so flourishing. But the heavy hand of the new régime was soon felt. The freely elected Legis-lative Assembly met on January 18; but its members were dismissed to their homes the very next day, when it became evident that the supporters of the Bolshevik revolution were in the minority. The 'Extraordinary Committee for the Suppression of Counter-revolution and Speculation,' or Cheka, was utterly ruthless in crushing the slightest sign of opposition; the Peace of Brest-Litovsk once concluded, Trotsky turned his unlimited energy to building up the Red Army, thus enabling the new State to defeat the approaching Tsarist forces one after another.

On March 11, 1918, the Soviet Government was transported by special train to Moscow, now restored to its old dignity as sole capital of the empire. Lenin had even followed another great national tradition by allowing the Metropolitan of Moscow to be crowned as Patriarch of the whole Russian Church (December 1, 1917). Notwithstanding this event a brutal persecution of the faithful soon began, marked by the slaughter of numbers of priests and accompanied by crude atheistical propaganda.

At the end of December 1922 the Russian Soviet Federation combined with the other, nominally independent, Communist States of the Russian colonial empire to form the Union of Soviet Socialist Republics; and by the time Lenin was forced out of political life by paralysis, shortly followed by his death on January 21, 1924, his régime could be said to have surmounted the worst of its initial difficulties.

PETROGRAD BECOMES LENINGRAD

Petersburg was particularly hard hit by the distresses that resulted from war and revolution. The transfer of the highest officials to Moscow reduced it to the status of deserted provincial town. In 1920 its population had fallen to 722,200, hardly a third of the pre-war figure. The stucco was peeling off its elegant buildings, grass was growing in the streets and squares, most of the shops had closed; in September 1924 the Neva flooded its banks, doing considerable damage, and the art treasures in the Hermitage had to be removed to a safer place.

On April 22, 1920, Peter the Great's city had been renamed after Lenin, which in itself was tantamount to a pledge on behalf of the Soviet economic planning. Within a few years the port had recovered its pre-war activity, and in the drive for the industrialization of the country the big factories around Leningrad, as the most important group of such undertakings already in existence, played a leading part. By 1926 the population had risen again to 1,614,000, and in 1939 it stood at 3,200,000—higher than the 1914 figure.

The second world war came as a new setback, but brought added prestige. On September 8, 1941, Hitler's troops, which had entered Russia on June 22, reached the outskirts of Leningrad. The siege of the city and its ultimate rescue from the German clutches are among the proudest memories left to the Soviet people by the war.

MOSCOW AS THE SOVIET CAPITAL

When the Soviet Government first moved into the Kremlin, Moscow too was in a pitiable condition. The middle classes, after long deluding themselves with the hope that the Soviet régime would collapse as rapidly as it had arisen, were decimated with cold-blooded cruelty and sank into utter misery. In 1920 the population had fallen to 1,000,000; scarcely more than half the 1915 figure. But recovery was more rapid here than anywhere, and soon carried the city to unprecedented develop-ment; and today the inhabitants number 5,000,000—probably more

PLATES 35–7. Moscow, the Kremlin.

PLATE 35. The main doorway of the Ouspiensky Cathedral, with its frescoes.

PLATE. 36. The front of the 'Faceted Palace' (Granovitaia Palata), overlooking the Cathedral Square. This palace, in whose throne-room part of the coronation ceremony used to take place, was built for Ivan III in 1487–91 by Marco Ruffo and Pietro Solario, who drew inspiration from older Russian architecture.

PLATE 37. Between the Faceted Palace (*left*) and the Ouspiensky Cathedral comes a glimpse of the Cathedral of the Ordination (Poloshenia Ris), built in 1484–6 by architects from Pskov, and of the three Churches of the Redeemer 'behind the golden lattice' beside the Tsarina's Palace, built in 1678–81 by Russian architects.

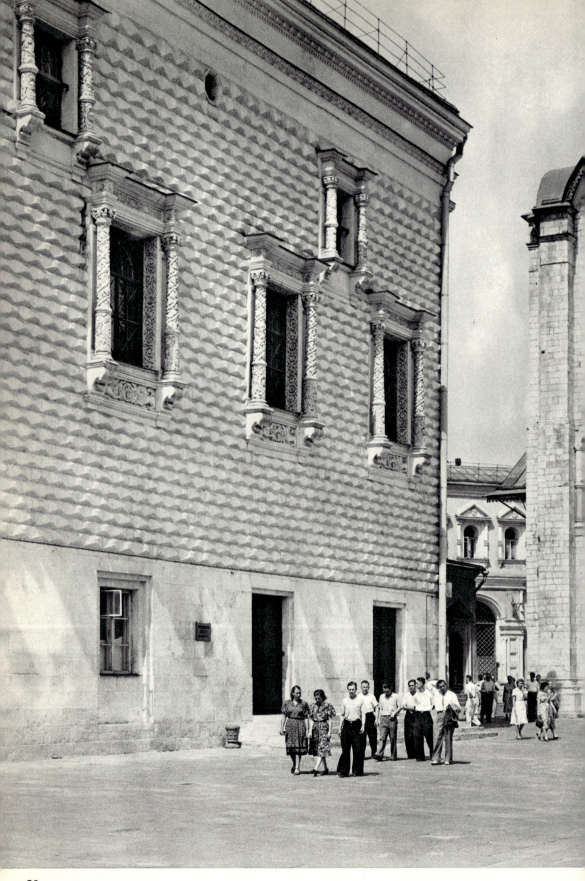

38

39

than 6,000,000 if the suburbs are included. As the capital of the U.S.S.R. and of its largest member, the Russian Soviet Federated Socialist Republic (R.S.F.S.R.) Moscow developed into a powerful centre of administration; for though the Federal aspect of the Soviet structure was constantly stressed, everything was in reality concentrated here, where all important political decisions were taken. Instructions went out from here to the Party, economic, cultural and military institutions of the whole Union, and here the strings that worked the Communist organizations in all parts of the world were gathered together. But Moscow's new rulers were determined that it should also serve as an example of Russia's development into a great industrial power, and a centre of heavy industry was built up here, the crucial year being 1930 whose achievements included the 'Elektrozavod' with its 20,000 workers, together with factories for the manufacture of trucks and lorries, ball bearings, instruments, etc. The Moscow region, with its ring of manufacturing towns—Vladimir, Ivanov, Yaroslavl, Kostroma, Ryazan and Tula—is now an industrial area with a population of some 20,000,000.

PLATES 38-9. Moscow, the Kremlin.

PLATE 38. In the Ouspiensky (Ascension) Cathedral, where the Tsars were formerly crowned and which is now a museum (cf. plates 23 and 36). The walls and the four pillars are covered with frescoes which used to be restored and extended at each coronation.

PLATE 39. The Armoury (Orujeinaia Palata) houses one of the richest museums in the whole country; among the masterpieces of Russian craftsmanship included in its collection —drawn from the treasure-chambers of the Great Princes of Moscow—is the ivory throne of Ivan III.

The industrialization of Moscow was comparatively far advanced before the urgent problem of housing was tackled on a comparable scale. After the revolution the victorious proletariat, a great proportion of which had hitherto been living in slums, took over the houses and flats of the middle classes; but even there they were hopelessly over-crowded, for the population was increasing at an alarming rate. It was not until about 1928 that the shanties and wooden houses of the working-class districts began to be replaced on something like an adequate scale by well-planned and properly equipped blocks of flats. Some buildings in the traditional style, started before the war, were completed at this time; but apart from these the glass and concrete constructions of European *avant garde* architecture seemed destined to triumph. This was the time when 'Battleship Potemkin' and other Russian films were being enthusiastically greeted by Western champions of novel, con-temporary art forms. The internationalism of the Communist move-ment seemed to be seeking expression in a style whose modernity appealed to the intellectuals of the capitalist countries in Europe as well. Le Corbusier, the highly ingenious exponent of functional architecture, submitted plans for one of the new public buildings and had prepared a further project on a magnificent scale. But by the time large-scale town-planning began, in the '30s, as an expression of the Soviet's confidence in its own power, the very different aesthetic standards of the Stalin era held sway.

In 1931 L. M. Kaganovich, then one of the leading figures in the Soviet Union, published a book on *The Socialist Reconstruction of Moscow and other Cities in the U.S.S.R.* and in July 1935 the Præsidium of the Party gave the signal that put his plans into execution. The task was not merely that of building houses, but of ensuring an ade-quate supply of water, electricity, gas and fuel, improving the drainage system, laying out streets and planning transport. In the 1920s 62 per cent of buildings in Moscow were made of wood and only 14 per cent of them were more than one storey high. But now great blocks of flats began to go up one after another. The city grew in concentric circles round the stately nucleus of the Kremlin. Wide streets now run from the centre in all directions, finally linking up with the ancient highroads that lead into the open country. On May 15, 1935, the first section of the underground railway was opened with considerable ceremony; this 'Metro', with its handsome stations, has since then been the special pride of the citizens, and is still being extended.

The development of Moscow was abruptly interrupted in the summer of 1941, when Hitler's tanks followed Napoleon's traces into Russia. From October to December the town was seriously threatened, and the Government moved for the time being to Kuybyshev. But the Soviet armies brought the fierce attack to a standstill at the outskirts of the city.

EXPERIENCING PRESENT-DAY MOSCOW

Emerging from our palatial hotel, we found ourselves in the centre of modern Moscow, where the earliest group of monumental buildings sprang up just before the general plan for the transformation of the city was launched in 1935. The towering stone façades of the official hotel and the ministerial building opposite are separated by the sixty-yard width of the Okhotny Riad. The name of this street recalls the hunts-men whose game was offered for sale here in the old days, before a lively general market grew on the spot. Modern development has swept away not only the picturesque old shops, tea-rooms, billiard saloons, restaurants and horse-cabs, but also the Spanish Gate (Iverskie Vorota), where the chapel with the famous ikon of the Spanish Madonna used to stand and through which one entered the Red Square.

The first stroll along the wide footpath of the Okhotny Riad, with its young lime trees, suffices to dispel our secret expectation of a com-pletely unfamiliar and somewhat sinister world. This is the central point of a great Empire, and its workaday face is calmly revealed to us.

The people hurrying past are doubtless occupied with more pressing concerns than their differences with the Western capitalist countries. In Moscow, as elsewhere, politics take up only a small share of life; problems such as food, lodging, clothing, wages, family matters, holiday plans, recreation and pleasures, work and personal relationships loom larger in the minds of these men and women, boys and girls. The fact that they are living in a Communist State does not cause them a second thought—for unlike the inhabitants of the so-called satellite countries, the present generation here has known no other form of government; only those over fifty-five can remember anything different.

They are dressed very much as we are, especially the men; as in other countries some are well clad and some shabby—though in this district, where the higher bureaucracy has its quarters, the better-dressed are in the majority. An occasional embroidered cap or Ukrainian shirt reminds

PLATES 40–3. Moscow, the Kremlin.

PLATE 40. The bell-tower in the Cathedral Square; left centre, the group of three buildings with the six-storey tower built by the Italian, Bono, in 1532–42. Here there hangs the chief bell of Moscow, which in the past used to give the signal that set the bells of all the city's 350 churches ringing on Easter night. On the right is the bell-tower of Ivan the Great (Ivan Veliky), erected during the famine of 1600 as part of the programme of public works introduced by Boris Godunov.

PLATES 41–2. The Tsar's Bell (Tsari kolokol) is believed to be the largest in the world; it weighs 200 tons. It was cast in 1735 by the bell-founder Motorin, who used metal from an older bell; but during a fire which broke out in 1737 it fell and was damaged.

PLATE 43. The Tsar's Cannon (Tsar Pushka), cast in 1586 by Tschechov, Master of the Royal Artillery, was always intended rather as a show-piece than as a weapon. It weighs 39 tons.

41

42

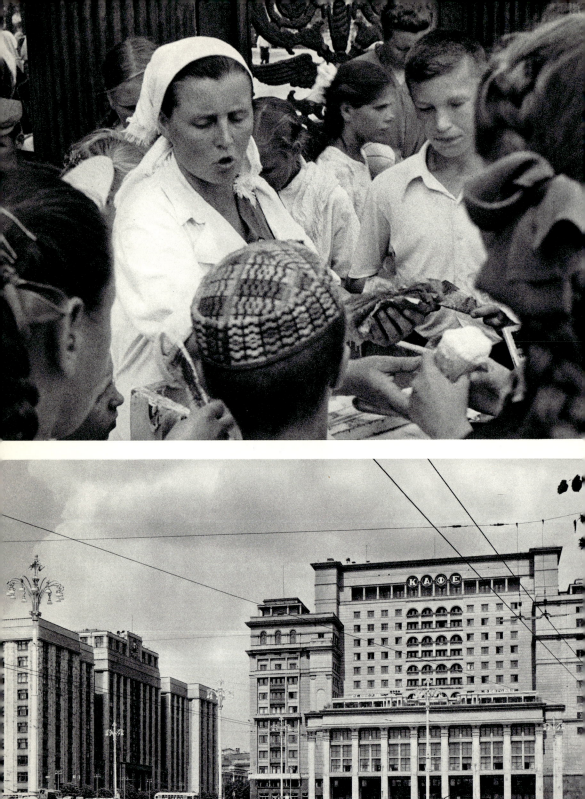

one of the traditional style of dress, but the familiar bourgeois aspect preponderates. Only the women look 'proletarian' to the Western visitor; the old-fashioned hats worn by a few of the younger ones are scarcely more attractive than the customary head-scarves, and elsewhere in Europe the brightly printed summer dresses would hardly find purchasers in the cheapest shop for mass-produced goods. Women can be seen here doing heavy street-repair work which in other countries is reserved for men. The 'insolently adorned vice' that shocked foreigners in the old days has vanished as completely as the once notorious filth and destitution. But a smiling face is a rare sight—we are in an orderly, serious, puritanical world. No one even turns to look at the picturesque figures who come out of the hotel—turbanned, bearded men from the Asian Soviet Republics, an elderly, bejewelled American woman with her husband, youthful, camera-laden Yankees in luridly patterned shirts, and people with every known colour of skin.

The stream of pedestrians takes little notice of the red lights at crossings and the cars—which are not very numerous—have to proceed cautiously. There are few bicycles and hardly any motorcycles. The chief means of transport is the long, single-decker bus, for which patient, disciplined queues wait at the stops. Dense crowds press in and out of the underground stations. The women selling ices at the street corners do steady

PLATES 44–5. Moscow.

PLATE 44. Ice-cream vendor on a hot summer day, outside the Moskva Hotel.

PLATE 45. Looking from the Alexander Gardens towards the Moskva Hotel. This showy building in the heart of the city was constructed in 1935 to a design by Shchusev, and enlarged in 1957; it stands at the point where the Spanish Gate used to lead from the food market in the Okhotny Riad into the Red Square. On the opposite side of the present-day Okhotny Riad stands the Soviet Cabinet building, also erected in 1935 (Architect, A. J. Langman).

93

business in this hot weather. Occasionally some ragged old woman may be seen covertly begging, usually in the evening outside a theatre.

A few paces from our hotel, round the corner of the sham-Gothic Historical Museum, and we are in the famous Red Square, the scene of so much bloodshed, so many processions and parades. To our right runs the Kremlin wall with its towers; in front of it the Lenin Mausoleum—whose severe cubist form dates from the early days of Bolshevik architecture—and the stands from which distinguished guests watch the May Day processions; to our left the long frontage of the one-time 'Torgsin', and in the background the fantastic Cathedral of St Basil, founded by Ivan the Terrible, with its central dome surrounded by assymetrically arranged cupolas which were only recently (1954) restored to the barbaric splendour of their original colour-scheme. At certain times the line of visitors—up from the provinces—waiting to pass through the mausoleum stretches right round the corner into the Alexander Park bordering the west wall of the Kremlin. The Red Flag flies from the

PLATES 46–50. Moscow.

PLATES 46–7. Passers-by in the Manege Square, a central part of Moscow.

PLATES 48–50. The Red Square.

PLATE 48. The east side, with the arcade of shops built in 1888–94 by Pomeranzew in a neo-Russian style, to replace the tradesmen's booths of medieval Moscow. The Upper Arcade (to the left of the picture) was rearranged in 1953 as the premises of GUM—the biggest multiple store in the Soviet Union. To the right, the Cathedral of St Basil.

PLATE 49. Looking north, where the Square is bounded by the neo-Gothic building of the Historical Museum, opened in 1883.

PLATE 50. Schoolchildren on a visit to the Red Square.

48

dome of the one-time Senate House, which rises above the wall, and the gilded, two-headed eagle of Byzantium has been replaced at the summit of each tower by a ruby-gleaming star.

The visitor armed with the necessary permit is admitted to the Kremlin through the western entrance, on the far side from the Tower of the Redeemer through which the official limousines of the Soviet leaders and their guests drive in. The buildings and open spaces enclosed by the mile and a half of wall, together with the garden on the southern side, form a carefully tended public site. The most important conferences and receptions are held in the great Kremlin Palace, which faces towards the river. At the centre lies the Cathedral Square, with its five churches and the palace of Ivan the Terrible—the most magnificent group of buildings in the whole of ancient Russia. Here, too, the most scrupulous restoration has recently been carried out; the lofty domes and the peaks of the towers are freshly gilded and a cross gleams from each of them— here in the innermost sanctum of a materialistic power. The days of open atheist propaganda are long past, and the patriotic war played its part in creating respect for the churches as architectural treasures and elements in the great national tradition, worthy of expert care—though Communism has abated nothing of its anti-religious claim to consti- tute the apex of human development. Like most Orthodox Greek churches, these cathedrals are comparatively small; the celebrated

PLATES 51–2. Moscow.

PLATE 51. A large triple apartment-block on one of the highways leading out of the city—built during the expansion that followed the second world war. The composer Shostakovich lives in the building on the left, which forms the pendant to the house in the right foreground.

PLATE 52. One of the blocks that have sprung up since 1950 around the new University building on the Lenin Hills; most of them are occupied by professors.

Ouspiensky Cathedral, for instance, measures 26 by 39 yards and is 42 yards high; its walls are covered with frescoes and the wealth of missals and holy vessels once used in its services is now displayed in show-cases lit by electric candles. In the Archangelsky Cathedral, with its wall paintings and portraits of the Tsars, explanations are provided by a rather obtrusive loudspeaker.

A stream of visitors, including deputations from all corners of the Soviet Union and an occasional Intourist group, makes a rather cursory inspection of these marvels; special attractions are the Great Bell, weighing over 200 tons, and the enormous imperial cannon cast in 1586. In the former armoury, built by the German architect Christoph Konrad in 1702–36, the treasures accumulated by rulers and Patriarchs through five centuries are on exhibition: incomparable crucifixes, chalices and other late medieval goldsmiths' work, crowns, ceremonial robes and weapons, gilded state coaches and sledges, an ivory throne, gifts presented to the Tsars by foreign potentates—from Sèvres porcelain and the choicest English silverware to the delicate masterpieces of Persian and Turkish craftsmen—and finally a golden model railway, jewelled clockwork figures and other toys devised for the last emperors.

The former Domskoi Monastery, whose church dates from the sixteenth century, contains a little architectural museum with a library, where we found a well-informed guide who took us to visit some examples of ancient Russian architecture which have survived outside the Kremlin. The seventeenth and eighteenth-century cathedrals, whose slender towers and bulb-shaped domes once rose far above the surrounding roofs, are now hidden among eight or ten-storey blocks. Several historical buildings I hoped to see on the strength of a 1929 guidebook had been sacrificed to the town-planning operations. Some of the churches preserved by the State as interesting monuments are also open for

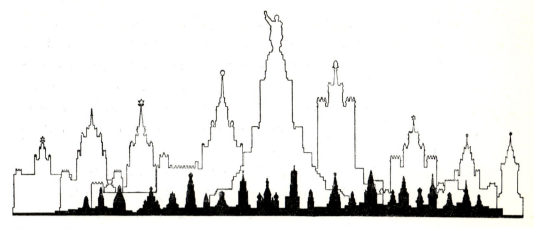

Moscow skyline—ancient and modern.

religious services; the remaining churches, and the clergy themselves, depend on voluntary contributions from their congregations. The majority of church-goers are old and, to judge by appearances, impoverished women; but one of my companions visited an ancient place of pilgrimage at some distance from Moscow, to find that crowds were pressing in to see its sacred ikons and that a great number of monks— young as well as old—lived in its cloisters.

The new blocks of flats are built in the style current in Europe at the turn of the century, and look definitely old-fashioned. A strange contrast is provided by sudden glimpses of the Ministry for Light Industry and Textiles, designed by Le Corbusier, and other isolated examples of the 'constructivist style' which originated in the 1920s. As new landmarks, there are already seven skyscrapers, including the Foreign Ministry, the new University and two hotels; their construction was decided in 1947, and according to the reconstruction plans for the period 1951–60 they are to form the nucleus of a series of others.

Around the huge University building on the Lenin Hills—formerly the Sparrow Hills—to the west of the city, a new residential district is nearing completion; ten-storey blocks interspersed with big courtyards where gardens are being laid out to relieve the oppressive effect of the massive stone buildings. Once the ancient city has been surrounded by the ring of new suburbs for which the present scheme makes provision, Moscow will not be allowed to grow any further. Beyond its boundaries there are later to be smaller, self-contained towns with little houses— probably something like the 'garden cities' so far known chiefly in England.

The enormous new University is entirely given over to the Faculty of Science, which has about 10,000 students. The classical Faculties are still housed in the old building to the west of the Kremlin. About 22,000 students live in Moscow. The new skyscraper, built in 1949–53, includes a hostel with 6,000 single rooms and 2,000 double rooms for students and 184 flats for professors; after scaling an impressive flight of steps to the pompous north doorway, one is astonished to find oneself in a cramped, ill-lit hall reminiscent of a barracks.

To the north the University buildings are bounded by a terrace; this is the spot from which Napoleon had his first glimpse of Moscow. The Moskva River flows at the foot of the hills, after describing a wide curve

PLATES 53–4. Moscow.

PLATE 53. Skyscraper in Smolensky Square, seen from across the Moskva River. This building, designed by Vladimir Gelfreich and Michail Minkus and completed in 1952, houses the Soviet Foreign Ministry and Ministry of Foreign Trade; its twenty-seven storeys contain about 2,000 offices, a conference hall to seat 500, and other rooms, twenty-eight lifts, four escalators, and a telephone switchboard with 400 lines.

PLATE 54. View from the terrace in front of the University on the Lenin (Sparrow) Hills, showing the Moskva River, part of the new sports ground, and the city with its towering new skyscrapers; in the centre of the right-hand page is the Novodievitzi Convent.

55

56

round the old part of the city. In the middle of the background the golden domes of the Kremlin cathedrals gleam through the mist. The foreground is occupied by a great new stadium. Against the distant skyline tower the white skyscrapers, the cathedrals of a materialistic era.

An endless succession and wide variety of conferences and political and cultural events helps to enhance the prestige of the Soviet capital. Each Republic in the Union is given the use of the Bolshoi Theatre and other institutions for ten days every two or three years, so that it can present its new operas, ballets, symphonies and plays. The ballet is as popular as ever and the standard for which it was famous in Tsarist days has been maintained. But drama and music, in obedience to general cultural policy, follow strictly conservative patterns—and call forth only moderate applause from their audiences. Seldom do we experience such originality on the stage and such spontaneous enthusiasm among the spectators as are to be found in Sergei Obrastzov's Marionette Theatre.

PLATES 55–6. The 'M. V. Lomonosov' Moscow State University, on the Lenin Hills, is an enormous group of buildings covering a total area of about 790 acres. A team of leading Soviet architects worked on the project from 1948–53. The principal building—thirty-one storeys high, with a central tower rising to 786 feet—contains the Geological and Geographical Faculties, the lecture-rooms of the Faculties of Mechanics and Mathematics, a hall to seat 1,500, museums, and the eleven-storey library. In front of the southern façade stands the memorial to Michail Vassilievich Lomonosov (1712–65), founder of Moscow University—a bronze statue by Tomski.

A visit to a Pioneer camp is something that no guest of Moscow can omit. The Pioneer organization was founded by Lenin in 1922, and almost all children between nine and fourteen belong to it. The cluster of wooden huts we saw, in a wood of firs and birches, was one of over a thousand, where boys and girls from Moscow can go for a fortnight in the summer. There are workshops where they can follow up their hobbies, and each team has its 'Soviet' as a preparation for future civic life. The children themselves seemed to have fresh, uninhibited personalities of their own.

Another place that should not be missed, especially by the art enthusiast, is the village of Kolomenskoie, on the Moskva River, some seven miles away from the capital. It is reached by an uneven country road running through a wide stretch of the Russian landscape with

PLATES 57–60. Kolomenskoie, on the Moskva River, about seven miles outside the city, was the summer residence of the seventeenth-century Tsar Alexei Mikhailovich. On the outskirts of the village an 'architectural park' has now been laid out, surrounding some fine examples of ecclesiastical architecture that remained from former times.

PLATE 57. The Church of the Resurrection, dating from 1532, with the tent-shaped roof above its dominating central tower, is one of the most striking examples of this early form of Russian church.

PLATE 58. The seventeenth-century portal leading to the group of churches.

PLATE 59. The log-house, brought from Marken Island, in which Peter the Great lived in 1702, while occupied in building up the Russian fleet.

PLATE 60. An example of ancient Russian wooden building, brought here from the north—a church built at Archangelsk in 1690.

which we are familiar from the great novels and which has scarcely altered in the course of centuries. The village consists of single-storey wooden cottages lying around a pond. Not far beyond it stands a group of churches, near which was the site of Tsar Alexei Mikhailovich's hunting-lodge; one of them, the Church of the Resurrection (1532) is among the finest examples of ancient Russian architecture. In the seventeenth century the second Romanov built himself a wooden palace nearby; it was pulled down only a hundred years later, but the entrance and yet another church still remain from his time. This idyllic spot has now become a kind of architectural reserve, where two historical wooden buildings from the north have been re-erected—a 1690 church and its tower, from the Archangelsk district, and the simple log-house from Marken Island in which Peter the Great lived in 1702 while founding the Russian navy.

LENINGRAD

A comfortable train journey takes us by night from Moscow to Leningrad.

In any discussion of fine architecture during our Moscow days, some-one was sure to tell us that we should discover the real thing in Leningrad —or Petersburg, as it is sometimes inadvertently called even nowadays. Under Soviet rule the positions of the two cities have been reversed,

PLATE 61. In the village of Kolomenskoie—an old barn, and beside it a house, recently erected in the traditional style of the district round Moscow.

PLATE 62. A well in a village west of Moscow.

Moscow developing vigorously and amid great publicity, while Leningrad, for two centuries the forum where all new ideas were threshed out, has gradually sunk back into the status of a well-kept museum. True, it has its industrial and residential suburbs and its great Kirov Stadium; but its historical centre has remained unchanged from the Petersburg days. Coming from Moscow is like leaving the nerve-centre of a great modern empire and arriving in an old-style royal residence.

Even the dictatorship of the proletariat has a weakness for traditional ways of life. The thickly carpeted corridors of the Hotel Astoria, the chandeliers and lamps, the ladies in charge of the room-keys on each floor—the entire service, in fact, testifies to the care instilled during the epoch of the Grand Dukes. The square outside our quarters is dominated by the elegantly arrogant equestrian statue of Nicholas I; nearby stands the Cathedral of St Isaac, a Palladian building topped by a pillared lantern supporting a dome—a masterpiece of Franco-Russian classical architecture now in process of restoration. Elsewhere the fine prospect of squares and quays shows hardly a trace of the damage done

PLATES 63–4. The 'Pioneer Camp' of Soya Kosomdenjanskaia is one of perhaps a thousand similar places, at varying distances around Moscow, to which the members of certain industries or vocational groups can go for rest and recreation. During the three summer months this particular camp is occupied each month by 250 'Pioneers'—members of the youth organization founded by Lenin—and 220 small children, all belonging to the families of the 3,000 employees of an iron and steel works.

PLATES 65–6. Pedestrians going past the Hotel Moskva in the centre of the city.

PLATE 67. One of the numerous whitewashed statues of youthful athletes produced in the academic style that prevails in the Soviet Union. Outside a public building in the Okhotny Riad.

65

66

67

by German bombs during the siege. The delicately tinted house-fronts on either side of the broad Neva, beneath the clouds that drift in from the sea, form a picture worthy of Canaletto—the yellow Admiralty building with the golden spike topping its entrance-tower; the pale green cluster forming the Winter Palace where the tragic events of 1905 and 1917 occurred; the crescent-shaped Military Headquarters building; the famous monument to Peter the Great, charging on horseback over a cliff towards the sea; and on the opposite bank, the slender turrets of the Fortress of Peter and Paul, the rostral columns of the Strelka, and the façades of yet more palaces. Houses and pavements give a rather more neglected impression as we stroll through the backstreets of the old district along the Griboiedov Canal; near the Lion Bridge we discover an idyllic, tree-shaded spot where time seems to have stood still for decades.

A visit to the Hermitage is a unique experience. Moscow and Leningrad have other first-class museums, such as the Tretiakov Gallery (Moscow) and the Russian Museum (Leningrad), without which one can form no adequate idea of Russian art; but the treasures of the former imperial collection in the Hermitage have a glamour that is all their own. Those of them for which space can be found are now exhibited in the numerous salons of the Winter Palace, while the caryatid portico of the old museum building next door remains closed. Here we are surrounded by the most sublime examples of European

PLATE 68. On the Lenin Hills outside Moscow, where the new University stands, ten-storey blocks of flats are going up side by side, bordering the open plain.

PLATE 69. The Kirov Stadium, which holds 100,000 spectators—part of the great sports ground laid out near Leningrad in 1952.

art, from the goldsmiths' work, miniatures and ivory Madonnas of the French Gothic period to Rembrandt's 'Prodigal Son'. There is a breath-taking display of objects from the tombs of Scythian princes, excavated in the last twenty or thirty years—gold by the hundredweight in the form of jewellery, vessels, stags and other animals. And the latest finds in the sphere of early central Asian civilizations, which were preserved intact in the ice of the Altai mountains. Russian visitors come in large numbers, and one somehow has the impression that there is more spontaneous interest, more individual enthusiasm and fewer officially organized parties here than in Moscow. It also seemed to us that the audiences in the two Opera Houses of Leningrad were more keenly interested and applauded more warmly than at the Bolshoi. Unlike the capital, Leningrad makes a surprisingly European impression.

THE SUMMER RESIDENCES OF THE TSARS

During our stay in Leningrad we almost forgot that we were in Soviet Russia; for even in Tsarist times we should presumably have been led to

PLATES 70–4. Leningrad.

PLATE 70. The Griboiedov Canal (formerly the Ekaterinsky Canal) runs through old Petersburg. In the background is the Church of the Resurrection, built in 1883–1907 on the spot where Alexander II was killed by a terrorist bomb in March 1881.

PLATES 71–4. Façade and interior of a station on the Leningrad underground, opened in 1955. The passages connecting the two platforms of every station, which lie far below ground level, are magnificently decorated with carefully selected marble of various kinds. Plate 74 shows a memorial to Pushkin which stands at the far end of one of the halls.

visit the same piously preserved monuments of Russian culture. One excursion took us 18 miles south of the city, to the erstwhile imperial summer residence, Tsarskoye Selo. Peter the Great presented the village of Sarskoe, on what was then Finnish territory, to his consort, Catherine, when it was renamed 'Tsar's Village'. In 1724 Rastrelli erected the 'Old Palace' in the most exuberant Russian baroque style, and the place was favoured both by the Empress Elizabeth and by Catherine II, the latter of whom further beautified the large park and had a second palace built. The Bolsheviks first called the place Dietskoe Selo—the Children's Village—but changed it again in 1937 to Pushkino, in honour of Russia's most popular poet. The school where Pushkin was a boarder from 1811–17 has been restored and was opened as a museum in 1949; visitors are shown the hall where Alexander I himself performed the opening ceremony in 1811, and the small rooms allotted to the 30 selected pupils. The Old Palace is still in a ruinous condition; but the park, with its pools and pavilions, has recovered the full beauty of the days when its royal owners played at an Arcadian existence there.

The other imperial residence we visited was Petrovoriets, the former Peterhof, on the southern coast of the Gulf of Finland. After founding St Petersburg, Peter the Great built himself a Versailles here; the palace, with its view over the sea, was erected by Leblond in 1711–17; Peter

PLATES 75–6. Leningrad.

PLATE 75. A typical corner of old Petersburg—the Lion Bridge, at a bend in the Griboiedov Canal.

PLATE 76. A park in the centre of the city, whose lavish display of baroque statues has been carefully restored.

himself lived in the little château of Monplaisir; Catherine II and the nineteenth-century Tsars added further buildings in the extensive park. The statues in the fountains have been repaired and re-gilded after the war-time damage and the fountains themselves are all playing. The hordes of present-day visitors share the childish pleasure taken by its imperial designers in this baroque park, with its unexpected vistas, tricks of per-spective, and hydraulic pleasantries such as the occasional stone which

PLATE 77. Peterhof, now known as Petrovoriets, was built as a summer residence for Peter I after the foundation of Petersburg. The Tsar lived in the modest little Château Monplaisir, which is built in the style of a Dutch country house, while the showy Great Palace was being constructed under his supervision, to the plans of Leblond (1711–17). It was to be further enlarged by Rastrelli in 1750. From the terraces in front of the palace the water flows down, through a series of fountains, to the shore of the Gulf of Finland.

PLATES 78–9. In the park of Peterhof (Petrovoriets): the chessboard cascade and one of the pools that lie to either side of the Grand Cascade.
This park was adorned during the eighteenth century with great numbers of fountains, statues and pavilions. In the autumn of 1941 it fell into the hands of the Germans, and by the end of the war it had been to a great extent laid waste. It has since been carefully restored, on the basis of the original plans; 125 fountains were brought into play again, and some 200 statues reconstructed.

PLATES 80–2. In the park at Peterhof.

PLATE 80. View from a bridge over the marine canal, towards the Great Palace and the Grand Cascade; centre, the Samson Fountain, whose jet of water rises to a height of 65 feet.

PLATE 81. The Adam Fountain.

PLATE 82. Looking from the terrace of the Great Palace, across the Grand Cascade and the marine canal, towards the sea.

81

83

84

when trodden on, releases a stream of water over the unsuspecting passer-by. The climax of all this is the series of cascades leading from the chief castle to the shore; the water flows down past gold-glittering statues into a great basin and thence along a central canal into the sea.

APOTHEOSIS BELOW THE GROUND

A visit to the Leningrad underground railway reveals Soviet art at its most ambitious. The first section was opened in 1955. At each station a moving staircase as long as that of the deepest London Tube leads down to two platforms separated by a brightly lit corridor, with a monumental work of art at either end—a mural painting of Stalin, arm

PLATES 83-4. At Pushkino, formerly Tsarskoye Selo, Peter I laid out an Orangerie and a zoological garden. His successors, particularly Catherine II, developed the place into a splendid summer residence, which was also a favourite with the last Tsars.

PLATE 83. Garden frontage of the great imperial palace named after Catherine II, which was built and choicely decorated during the reigns of the Empress Elizabeth and Catherine II.

PLATE 84. A pavilion in the extensive park.

PLATE 85. A nursery school in the summer camp of a Moscow factory (see plates 63-4).

PLATE 86. The new University of Moscow, on the Lenin Hills.

PLATE 87. Driving westward towards Moscow, across the desolate plain, one's first glimpse of the city is provided by the fantastic outline of the new University, lit up by the rays of the setting sun.

raised and eye flashing prophetic fire, giving orders for socialist construction, a gigantic bust of Lenin, or a statue of Pushkin. There are walls faced with many-coloured, highly polished marble, skilful direct or indirect lighting, bas-reliefs and decorations of gilded bronze in which hammer and sickle, oak leaf and Soviet star continually recur. In the station reserved by our interpreter for the final visit, the pillars were covered with bas-reliefs in coloured glass, massive chandeliers reflected their lights in the marble paving, and a touching mosaic picture, lit by projectors, announced 'Peace on Earth'. Returning, full of conflicting impressions, to our own world, we may perhaps venture to add 'and Goodwill to Men'.